The Quiet Gap: Understanding Fusion Centers and the Intelligence-Led Patrol Officer

The Quiet Gap: Understanding Fusion Centers and the Intelligence-Led Patrol Officer

Lloyd Nguyen, DBA

Table of Contents

Introduction

The Unfinished Promise of Intelligence Sharing

On an ordinary day, a patrol officer may notice something that doesn't look like a crime—at least not right away. A pattern of reports might seem unrelated. A brief contact with the wrong person might feel too small to matter. Most of the time, those small signals fade into routine. But after September 11, 2001, law enforcement agencies across the United States were asked to think differently. Terrorism threats didn't follow jurisdiction lines. Danger didn't wait for the "right" agency to connect the dots. The expectation shifted from simply responding to incidents to helping prevent harm through earlier awareness and coordinated action. That expectation gave rise to a new kind of partnership: fusion centers.

Fusion centers were built to help local agencies connect information, analyze risk, and share intelligence so that communities could be protected sooner and more effectively. Yet behind the policy language and interagency agreements lies a harder question—one that is rarely asked directly: Do local law enforcement personnel truly understand what fusion centers are for, and what their own agency is supposed to do within the system? Because if understanding is incomplete, intelligence sharing doesn't fail dramatically. It fails quietly. Information is delayed. Signals are misunderstood. Contributions are inconsistent. And the promised benefit—turning scattered signals into actionable threat awareness—doesn't fully arrive.

I spent 27 years in law enforcement, working in corrections, patrol, gang task force, terrorism liaison, and administration. In addition to law enforcement, I served four years on active duty in the United States Marine Corps and eleven years in the United States Air Force Reserve. While in the Marine Corps, I was deployed to the Middle East and participated in Operations Desert Shield/Desert Storm. After 9/11, I reenlisted in a different branch of service (USAFR) in support of the Global War on Terrorism.

Those decades gave me a front-row seat to how information moves—or doesn't—through the ranks. While pursuing my doctorate in Homeland Security, I read the 9/11 Commission Report and, through other research solidified for me what was missing in terms of intelligence-led policing. It was a lack of deliberate education about why the ordinary patrol officer matters to national intelligence efforts.

That recognition sharpened when I transitioned into the classroom, either teaching in-service law enforcement officers or criminal justice students who were on their way into law enforcement careers. I could see how easily the next generation could inherit the same gap unless someone built a bridge. The textbooks covered policy structure and legal frameworks. The academy trainers focused on physical skills and report writing. But the connective tissue, the mental model that turns a patrol officer into an active node in the intelligence network—was missing. I knew then that the gap was not a failure of will. It was a failure of curricular imagination.

This book is the result of that realization. It examines how the fusion center function is understood from the ground up, how agencies interpret their role in intelligence sharing, and what happens when homeland security reform expectations meet the day-to-day realities of policing. My doctoral dissertation draws directly on the perceptions of administrators and practitioners inside a local police agency—people who live the disconnect every shift. Their voices reveal something that policy documents rarely capture: the gap between what fusion centers promise and what patrol officers believe they are being asked to do.

The result is not just a description of a program. It's a map of how fusion centers live—or struggle to live—in practice. And it offers practical lessons for strengthening intelligence sharing in ways that can support homeland security policing while also accounting for civil liberties and privacy. What makes this story compelling is also what makes it important: fusion centers are only as effective as the understanding that powers them. The solution begins with teaching, and the classroom is where we can change the outcome before the first shift begins.

The Educator as the Critical Fulcrum

When I stepped into either a law enforcement training center or the college classroom, I carried a set of assumptions that didn't survive first contact with my students. I expected them to have at least a foundational grasp of how their future agencies would interact with fusion centers. Instead, I found intelligent, motivated people who understood the mission of federal homeland security agencies but couldn't explain what a suspicious activity report actually triggers inside a fusion center. They knew about terrorism threats in the abstract. They didn't know that their own patrol observations, the things they would see on traffic stops, building checks, and casual citizen contacts—were the raw material of intelligence analysis. That gap wasn't their fault. It was ours.

Criminal justice instructors, academy coordinators, and field training officers hold a unique lever that no policy directive can replicate. A policy tells officers what to do. Education tells them why it matters. When an officer understands why a particular observation deserves documentation, why seemingly minor data points matter when aggregated, and why fusion centers are structured as they are, the behavior changes at the cognitive level—not just the compliance level. That deeper shift is what separates intelligence-led policing from checkbox-driven reporting. And it starts in the learning environment, before badges are pinned on.

This book is written primarily for the educators and trainers who shape law enforcement thinking: No discussion of fusion centers and intelligence sharing can conclude without addressing the tension that hovers over the entire enterprise: the relationship between proactive information collection and civil liberties. This tension is real. It has generated lawsuits, public backlashes, and deep mistrust in some communities. An officer trained to notice and report suspicious patterns may, without careful guidance, drift into profiling based on constitutionally protected characteristics. That risk cannot be dismissed or minimized.

criminal justice professors building degree curricula, academy instructors designing basic training modules, and agency training coordinators preparing in-service programs. The chapters ahead offer a roadmap for integrating fusion center knowledge into educational settings, turning a policy concept into professional competency. I address patrol officers and administrators as well because their perspectives illuminate why education matters, but the core argument is strategic: the classroom is where the quiet gap gets closed or left open for another generation.

The book builds layer by layer, starting with a clear diagnosis of the problem—why fusion centers falter at the street level despite good intentions and significant investment. From there, it introduces the core principle of intelligence-led policing as a mindset that any patrol officer can adopt, rather than a specialized role reserved for off-site analysts. Practical training tools follow, including exercises, field guides, and administrative tactics that translate concepts into action. A chapter on recovery equips trainers to handle breakdowns, resistance, and high-profile mistakes without losing ground. Finally, we examine the long-term identity shift that transforms an occasional reporter into a career-long intelligence contributor.

Throughout these chapters, I return to a single conviction: fusion center effectiveness is an educational problem more than a technical one. Policy can mandate information sharing. Technology can facilitate it. But only teaching—deliberate, well-designed, context-rich teaching—can build the understanding that makes sharing consistent, accurate, and civil-liberties-conscious. The officers who report suspicious activity are the same officers who protect constitutional rights in their daily work. Proper education ensures they can do both with equal confidence, recognizing that intelligence-led policing and privacy protection are complementary commitments, not competing ones.

What you hold is not an academic exercise. It's a practical intervention. It's built from the ground up—from patrol cars to briefing rooms to college lecture halls—and shaped by the lived experience of people who know what's at stake when signals go unseen. The ordinary day of a patrol officer can either remain a routine blur or become a critical node in a protective network. The difference lies in what we teach, how we teach it, and whether we start before the first shift begins. That work begins now.

Chapter 1: The Problem – Why Fusion Centers Falter at the Street Level

The Unseen Disconnect

Dispatcher Jane shifted the phone to her other ear and re-keyed the radio for the third time in sixty seconds. The dispatcher's console glowed green and amber in the dim room, a quiet Thursday afternoon in a mid-sized city. Officer John had just cleared a suspicious person call with the same phrase he always used: "No action." Jane had heard the original call come in—a resident near the industrial park reporting a utility van parked outside a closed HVAC supplier, two men in reflective vests, one photographing the building. It wasn't a crime. It wasn't even odd, not really. Work trucks with guys in vests. Happens every day. But something tugged Jane's mind: third week in a row. Different vans, same block. She said nothing, filed nothing, and the call logged out with no flag.

A pattern that might have linked to staged commercial burglaries, or worse, to pre-operational surveillance—evaporated before it reached any analyst's desk. This is not a story of negligence. John is a good officer, careful and thorough, well-liked on his shift. Jane is a competent dispatcher. What they share is a quiet assumption that has eroded fusion center effectiveness for two decades: the belief that intelligence work is someone else's job. Fusion centers belong to joint terrorism task forces, to state analysts, and to the detectives who work in plainclothes and go to regional meetings. The patrol officer and the dispatcher are doers, not gatherers; responders, not reporters. The burden of connecting small signals falls elsewhere.

That assumption sits like silt at the bottom of the intelligence-sharing pipeline. When the nation's fusion centers were conceived after 9/11, the architects imagined a seamless flow: local observations feeding into regional analysis, producing threat awareness that circled back to the street. The design was sound. The policy frameworks, the technology platforms, and the interagency agreements were all built with care. What the architects underestimated was the human filter at the point of collection—the patrol officer standing beside a stopped vehicle, unsure whether what he noticed is worth documenting, deciding, in a split second and under competing demands, to let it go.

Research into fusion center utilization confirms this gap is not theoretical. Studies of local law enforcement agencies reveal a persistent pattern: officers who receive no formal training on fusion center functions report suspicious activity at significantly lower rates than those who do. More troubling, when officers are asked what a fusion center actually does with the information they submit, the answers range from vague to entirely wrong. Some believe the center is purely a terrorism watchlist, irrelevant to everyday policing. Others fear the center functions as internal affairs by another name—a monitoring body watching how police do their jobs. Neither belief is accurate, but both beliefs shape behavior.

The language used in fusion center outreach often deepens the disconnect. Bulletins arrive by email with subject lines like "Suspicious Activity Reporting Guidance" or "Nationwide SAR Initiative Update." The material is accurate, properly vetted, and almost entirely unread. A patrol sergeant with twenty-five officers to supervise, a shift briefing to run, and a stack of use-of-force reports to review does not prioritize a PDF titled "Enhancing the Baseline for Information Sharing." The message, however well-crafted, lands in a mental inbox marked Optional, Federal, Not My Problem.

And yet, fusion centers were never meant to be optional. The whole architecture of post-9/11 homeland security intelligence depends on the premise that local officers will serve as the nation's eyes and ears. These tripwires detect abnormal activity before it coalesces into a plot. The 2007 National Strategy for Information Sharing explicitly placed state, local, and tribal law enforcement at the center of the intelligence cycle. The strategy's language was unambiguous: fusion centers would succeed only if patrol officers understood their role and contributed willingly. A decade and a half later, the understanding remains thin.

What makes the disconnect particularly stubborn is that it is invisible to some agency leaders. Chiefs and sheriffs attend fusion center briefings, receive threat assessments, and may even sit on governance boards. They assume their officers know what they know. In my doctoral research, I found that in the perceptions of fusion centers, administrators consistently rated their agency's understanding of intelligence sharing higher than line officers did—sometimes by a wide margin. The gap between the chief's office and the patrol car is not just one of rank; it is one of shared awareness. The administrator sees the flow of reports coming out of the fusion center and thinks the system works. The officer on the street, who never sees what happens after a report is filed, thinks the system doesn't notice them at all.

This is not a problem that training bulletins can fix on their own, a point explored more fully when we turn to the training tools themselves. The problem goes deeper than information transfer. It is a problem of identity and culture—the patrol officer's sense of what the job includes and what it leaves to others. Until that changes, the fusion center will remain, as it is with too many agencies: a distant, somewhat important-sounding office that doesn't truly intersect with the daily work of responding to calls, writing reports, and going home at the end of a shift.

The Psychology of Small Signals

Consider a routine traffic stop on a Tuesday morning. A patrol officer pulls over a sedan for an expired registration. The driver is polite, almost rehearsed. In the back seat: two cans of a household cleaning chemical, a roll of thick-gauge wire, and a stack of city infrastructure maps. The officer runs the driver's license, writes the citation, and sends the car on its way. He notes the chemicals in his report as "items in plain view" but flags nothing further. It is not a crime to carry cleaning chemicals. It is not suspicious to have maps. Individually, each detail is inert. Together, they form a pattern that a trained analyst would recognize as a potential precursor to improvised explosive device assembly. But the patrol officer never connects the dots because he was never taught that connecting the dots is part of his job.

The psychology behind this filtering is well-documented in decision-making research. Human beings, including highly trained police officers, rely on heuristics—mental shortcuts—to manage the flood of sensory information they encounter. When an observation fits no preexisting mental category labeled "threat" or "intelligence," the brain discards it. The cleaning chemicals get classified as household items, the maps as directions, and the encounter as a routine traffic stop. The classification is efficient; it keeps the officer moving and keeps the shift on schedule. The classification is also how signals die.

What makes this filtering especially dangerous is that it compounds. One officer dismisses one observation. Another officer, three days later, encounters a related observation, perhaps a report of someone buying large quantities of the same chemical from a different store. That second officer also dismisses it. Neither officer knows about the other's encounter because neither filed a report that would allow a cross-reference. The fusion center analyst, who might have spotted the connection, never receives either data point. The system did not fail catastrophically. It failed quietly, one routine decision at a time.

This phenomenon is not limited to terrorism precursors. It applies across the intelligence spectrum. Human trafficking indicators—a young woman who doesn't speak, someone else holding her identification, a hotel room paid in cash for a week by a third party—are encountered by patrol officers every day and often written off as domestic disputes or prostitution arrests. Gang intelligence—graffiti that signals territorial expansion, unusual movement patterns near known conflict zones, the sudden appearance of out-of-state vehicles—flickers past officers who lack the framework to recognize it. The small signals are everywhere; the trained eye to catch them is not.

Compounding the psychology of dismissal is the officer's understandable fear of reporting incorrectly. No officer wants to be the one who filed a suspicious activity report that turned out to be nothing—or worse, that sparked a complaint. In a profession where credibility is currency, the risk of looking foolish, or being perceived as profiling, exerts a powerful chilling effect. The safer path is to file nothing. The safer path leads directly to the quiet gap.

There is also a temporal dimension. Patrol officers work at a rhythm of immediate resolution: a call comes in, the officer responds, the situation is resolved or handed off, the report is written, the call is cleared. Intelligence gathering operates on a different timeline. The value of a single suspicious activity report may not become apparent for weeks, months, or even years, as it sits in a database waiting to intersect with other reports from other agencies. That delayed return on investment makes no sense to an officer who measures a successful shift by the number of calls handled and incidents resolved. The reward structure of patrol work rewards closure. Intelligence work rewards patience. The two are in tension.

Breaking this psychological pattern requires more than a policy memo. It requires a deliberate effort to retrain the officer's mental model of what constitutes a "significant" observation—the core work of the training framework laid out later in this book. Officers need to experience, in concrete, memorable ways, how scattered fragments become actionable intelligence when collected, combined, and analyzed. Until they see the outcome of reporting—and until the fear of overreporting is addressed directly—the psychology of dismissal will continue to govern the street.

The Administrators' Perspective

Captain America walked out of the quarterly fusion center liaison meeting with a binder thick with threat bulletins and a quiet confidence that his department was doing its part. His agency, a county sheriff's office with roughly five hundred sworn personnel, had assigned a representative to attend these meetings regularly. Reports came back from the fusion center monthly. When the sheriff asked whether the department was integrated into the intelligence-sharing network, Captain America could answer honestly: yes. The boxes were checked. The relationships existed. What the captain did not know, because he had no mechanism for knowing, was that the flow of information from his patrol deputies to the fusion center had slowed to a trickle. Of the forty-two suspicious activity reports expected from his jurisdiction in the past year, eleven had been submitted. Not because deputies saw nothing, but because they did not recognize what they saw as reportable.

This is the administrator's blind spot: visibility into the fusion center system's outputs without corresponding visibility into the inputs from their own officers. The fusion center delivers polished threat assessments, well-formatted reports, and professional briefings. Those products create an impression of a functioning pipeline. The administrator sees the water coming out of the tap and assumes the plumbing is intact. What goes unseen is the narrowing of the pipe at the source, the patrol officer who never turned the valve.

The problem is partly structural. Some agency administrators may not track suspicious activity reporting as a performance metric. Arrests, response times, and clearance rates are tracked. These numbers appear in CompStat meetings, in annual reports, and in budget justifications. The number of intelligence reports filed by patrol officers rarely appear anywhere. What is not measured is not managed, and what is not managed gradually disappears from the organization's culture. Officers learn, without anyone ever saying it explicitly, that intelligence reporting is extracurricular—commendable perhaps, but not essential.

Administrators also face a messaging challenge they rarely recognize. When a chief or sheriff emphasizes fusion center participation, perhaps mentioning it at a command staff meeting or forwarding a threat bulletin with a brief note—the message travels downward through the ranks with diminishing force. The patrol officer at the end of the chain receives it as one more item in an endless stream of administrative directives. The message lacks context, urgency, and, most importantly, a clear articulation of what the officer is actually supposed to do differently on the next shift. A forwarded bulletin is not training. A mention at a staff meeting is not a culture change.

There is also a generational factor complicating the administrator's challenge. Many current police leaders began their careers before fusion centers existed. They learned policing in an era when intelligence was a detective function, not a patrol function. Their own career trajectories did not include the expectation that street officers would serve as intelligence collectors. That history shapes their assumptions about what patrol work includes, even as their rhetoric embraces intelligence-led policing. The subconscious model of the patrol officer—the one these leaders carry from their own time in uniform—predates the fusion center era. Aligning conscious policy with inherited mental models is slow, difficult work that rarely happens through directives alone.

The administrator's role in closing this gap is not primarily to issue more memos or attend more meetings. It is to change the institutional incentives that shape officer behavior, a subject addressed in detail in the Administrator's Playbook developed later. Until patrol officers see that their leaders genuinely value intelligence reporting—and back that value with training, performance metrics, and recognition—the gap between the chief's understanding and the officer's understanding will remain as wide as it is today.

Consequences of the Gap

The consequences of the quiet gap are not theoretical. In 2013, a twenty-year-old man walked into a shopping mall in a mid-sized American city and opened fire, killing two people before taking his own life. The subsequent investigation revealed a trail of indicators that preceded the attack by months: online postings threatening violence, the purchase of ammunition in unusual quantities, and two separate encounters with patrol officers—one during a domestic disturbance call, one during a suspicious vehicle check near the mall itself. In both encounters, the officers noted the man's agitated state but filed no intelligence report. The reports they did file—standard incident reports—went into the department's records management system, where they sat in isolation, disconnected from each other and from the broader threat picture. The fusion center analyst who later pieced the timeline together concluded that the indicators, taken collectively, would have triggered a threat assessment had any of them been submitted through the intelligence channel. The information existed. It simply never moved.

This pattern repeats across jurisdictions and threat types. A domestic extremism plot disrupted by the FBI in 2020 succeeded only because a patrol officer in a small Midwestern town filed a suspicious activity report after stopping a vehicle loaded with firearms, tactical gear, and handwritten notes referencing a government building. That officer had received fusion center training six months earlier. The difference between the near-miss and the prevented attack was not better technology or more analysts; it was a single officer who understood what he was looking at and took the extra step to report it through the intelligence system. For every such success, there are an unknown number of failures—signals that never surfaced, patterns that never formed, threats that progressed without interruption.

The consequences extend beyond public safety. When patrol officers do not understand the fusion center's function, the resulting underreporting skews the entire intelligence picture. Fusion center analysts work with the data they receive. If the data underrepresents certain geographic areas, types of threats, or patterns of precursor activity because officers in those areas are not reporting, the resulting threat assessments will have blind spots. The fusion center's analysis is only as good as its inputs, and its inputs are only as comprehensive as the officers who provide them. A fusion center that receives robust reporting from one jurisdiction and near-silence from its neighbor is, in effect, analyzing half the picture while believing it sees the whole.

An equally damaging but less visible consequence is the erosion of the partnership model itself. When patrol officers file reports that receive no feedback—when they submit a suspicious activity report and hear nothing back, month after month, year after year—they reasonably conclude the report was useless. From the officer's perspective, the fusion center is a black hole: information goes in, nothing comes out. That perception, accurate or not, is corrosive. It teaches the officer that intelligence reporting is a formality, a bureaucratic exercise that yields no operational benefit. The partnership that fusion centers were built to foster between local law enforcement and the intelligence community withers into a one-way obligation, resented rather than valued.

The cost in trust is perhaps the most durable consequence of all. When a high-profile event occurs—a mass shooting, a terrorist incident, a major human trafficking case—and the subsequent investigation reveals that law enforcement had encountered fragments of the threat but failed to connect them, the public's faith in the system erodes. The question becomes: why didn't someone piece this together? The answer is often not that no one could have. It is that the pieces were scattered among officers who did not recognize them as pieces, in agencies that had not built the internal culture to collect them. The fusion center, designed precisely to assemble those pieces, sat on the periphery of the officers' awareness, a resource they had heard mentioned but never truly understood.

Addressing these consequences demands more than incremental improvement. It demands a fundamental reconsideration of how patrol officers are taught to see their own observations and how agencies are taught to value intelligence reporting. The following chapters take up that challenge directly, beginning with the core framework that makes intelligence-led policing comprehensible to the person in the patrol car.

Why Training Alone Isn't Enough

A two-hour block of instruction on fusion center capabilities, delivered once at an in-service training day, will not close the gap. Neither will the laminated reference card, the emailed bulletin, nor the annual directive reminding officers to report suspicious activity. These interventions have been tried in countless agencies across the country, yielding modest results at best. The problem is not that the information is wrong. The problem is that the information sits atop a deeper structure—a set of cultural norms, professional habits, and institutional incentives—that actively discourages the behavior the training seeks to encourage. Training that does not address the underlying structure will wash away within weeks of returning to the street.

Consider what a patrol officer experiences after sitting through a fusion center orientation. The training session emphasizes the importance of reporting suspicious activity. The officer leaves the room with a vague sense of obligation but no clear mental image of what "suspicious" looks like in the specific context of intelligence gathering. The next shift, the officer stops a vehicle with a trunk full of electronics still in their packaging. Is that suspicious? Maybe. Or maybe it's just someone who went shopping. The officer hesitates, thinks of the paperwork, remembers the last time a report generated no response, and decides to clear the call. The training, however well-intentioned, did not survive contact with the ambiguity of real policing.

The bigger change that is required is cultural. In an agency that has genuinely integrated intelligence-led policing into its identity, patrol officers do not decide whether to report; reporting is part of the job, as automatic as calling out a traffic stop location or completing a use-of-force form. That kind of embedded behavior does not come from information sessions. It comes from repeated, reinforced practice over time, supported by supervisors who model the behavior, performance evaluations that reward the behavior, and agency leaders who communicate, in word and deed, that intelligence gathering is a core patrol function, not an add-on.

This book is built on the conviction that cultural change of this depth is achievable, but only through a deliberate, multi-layered approach that addresses the psychology, training, administrative structures, recovery mechanisms, and the identity transformation required. The next chapters lay out that approach, beginning with the core framework of intelligence-led policing and moving through practical tools, recovery strategies, and the long-term identity shift that makes the change permanent. The quiet gap can be closed. But closing it requires understanding it first—and the first step is recognizing that the gap is not a training deficit. It is a failure of shared understanding, and it will not be solved by any single intervention acting alone.

Chapter 2: The Core Principle – Intelligence-Led Policing (ILP) as a Patrol Officer's Mindset

What ILP Actually Means for the Street Officer

David had been out of the academy for eleven months when he pulled over a sedan with rental plates and a driver who seemed far too calm. The trunk held camera equipment, a police scanner, and hand-drawn diagrams of a water treatment facility—but no law had been broken. David let the driver go with a warning for rolling through a stop sign. He didn't file a report because, in his mind, there was nothing to report. That decision wasn't negligence; it was the natural outcome of a career spent learning that police work means responding to incidents, not collecting fragments of information that don't add up to a crime.

Intelligence-led policing asks officers to make a subtle but profound shift: to see themselves not only as responders but as sensors. This doesn't mean turning patrol officers into intelligence analysts or asking them to surveil communities. It means recognizing that the raw material of threat awareness, the odd question, the strange rental, the out-of-place visitor—flows through the patrol officer's daily contacts long before it reaches anyone with an analyst's title. The officer who understands this doesn't need to connect the dots themselves; they need to recognize when a dot is worth reporting so someone else can connect it.

For department leadership, the challenge is defining ILP in terms that make sense to a patrol officer on a twelve-hour shift; abstract invocations of "homeland security" or "information sharing" land flat. What lands is this: your observations are the front edge of a system designed to catch threats before they become crimes—and the system is blind without you. ILP, stripped of policy jargon, is the disciplined practice of noticing, documenting, and passing along what doesn't fit.

The shift from reactive to proactive isn't binary; it happens on a spectrum. At the most basic level, an ILP-minded officer reports suspicious activity that they would previously have dismissed. At a more advanced level, they begin to recognize baseline patterns in their patrol area—which vehicles belong, which rhythms are normal—and notice deviations without being prompted. Neither level requires the officer to conduct analysis; both levels require the officer to believe their observations have value beyond the immediate call.

This belief doesn't emerge from memos. It emerges from seeing the loop close: an officer submits a suspicious activity report about someone photographing bridge supports, and weeks later, a supervisor mentions that the report was combined with three others from neighboring jurisdictions to identify a reconnaissance pattern. The officer doesn't need to see the full analysis; they need to see that their piece mattered. Closing the feedback loop is an administrative responsibility that will be explored more fully later, but its absence is often what causes ILP to stall before it starts.

What ILP is does not matter as much as what it is. It is not a surveillance program aimed at communities or individuals based on religion, ethnicity, or political activity. It is not a backdoor for federal agencies to direct local policing priorities. It is not a quota system demanding a set number of intelligence reports per shift. When these misconceptions take hold—whether among officers or the public, the result is resistance that undermines the entire effort. Clear definitions, delivered early and reinforced often, are the first line of defense against this corrosion.

The street officer who understands ILP correctly gains something beyond professional relevance: they gain a framework that makes their job more coherent. The random encounters that once felt like loose ends—the nervous tenant, the abandoned storage unit, the too-specific questions at the hardware store—become pieces of a larger picture. The work doesn't change. The meaning of the work does.

The Fusion Center as a Partner, not a Monitor

Among patrol officers, suspicion of fusion centers often runs deeper than ignorance; it carries the edge of distrust. Who is reading these reports? What are they doing with the information? Are they tracking us or the public? These questions aren't paranoid, they reflect a structural reality in which patrol officers are asked to send information into a system they cannot see, to people they have never met, with no guarantee of what happens next. The absence of relationships breeds the assumption of surveillance, and that assumption chills reporting before it begins.

The corrective is not a policy directive but a partnership model. A fusion center that sends an analyst to ride along with patrol officers for a single shift builds more trust than a year of interagency agreements. When an officer watches an analyst receive a seemingly trivial report—a stolen delivery truck, a falsified hazmat endorsement—and hears the analyst explain how that report connects to five others in the region, the fusion center stops being an abstraction. It becomes a room full of people whose work depends on what the officer sees.

This partnership must be structured as a two-way exchange. Intelligence doesn't only flow up from the street to the center; it must flow back down. Officers need to receive fusion center products relevant to their patrol areas: trends in cargo theft, patterns of fraudulent document use, and indicators of pre-operational surveillance tied to local infrastructure. These products don't need to be classified as intelligence briefs; they need to be concise, actionable, and delivered at shift briefings in language the officer can use immediately. When the fusion center consistently provides value, the officer's willingness to reciprocate increases naturally.

The partnership model also requires fusion centers to understand the operational constraints of patrol work. An officer who is asked to fill out a lengthy intelligence report after every suspicious contact will stop reporting entirely—not out of resistance, but out of sheer pressure on time. Fusion center personnel who have never worked patrol often underestimate how quickly discretionary tasks disappear under the weight of calls for service. A practical partnership designs reporting mechanisms that are fast, mobile-friendly, and integrated into existing documentation workflows rather than bolted on as an additional burden.

Trust, once built, must be maintained through consistency. An officer who submits a detailed report and never hears acknowledgment will eventually conclude that the effort was wasted. An analyst who receives a stream of irrelevant tips from an untrained officer may start ignoring that officer's submissions. The partnership model works only when both sides see the other as a reliable counterpart; when patrol officers trust that their reports are read. Analysts trust that patrol officers are reporting with purpose. This mutual reliability is not a natural condition; it is cultivated, requiring deliberate attention from supervisors on both ends.

Where this partnership functions well, the cultural divide between "the street" and "the center" narrows. Officers begin to speak of "our analysts" rather than "the fusion center." Analysts begin to answer their phones knowing the caller is an officer with a question, not a complaint. The intelligence system becomes human, and human systems—unlike bureaucratic ones—tend to work.

Reporting vs. Surveillance: The Critical Distinction

The most corrosive fear surrounding intelligence-led policing is that it turns patrol officers into agents of surveillance—watching communities, profiling individuals, feeding a government database with information scraped from daily life. After 9/11, the fear is based on observing a specific group of people. In my research, consistent literature has warned homeland security authorities to be cautious to not violate the Establishment Clause of the First Amendment when observing a community's religious beliefs and practices. Any ILP framework that ignores this issue may face dire constitutional consequences as communities will resist cooperating. The framework must therefore draw a bright, unmistakable line between reporting and surveillance.

Reporting targets patterns and behaviors, not people. An officer who notices that an individual is photographing security checkpoints, taking notes on guard rotations, and returning to the same location at odd hours is observing behavior—conduct that, in context, may indicate pre-operational planning. That same officer, if they were to begin tracking the individual's movements without cause, building a file on their associations, or monitoring their lawful activities based on their identity or beliefs, would have crossed the line into surveillance. The distinction is not merely legal; it is operational. Reporting asks: What is this person doing that doesn't fit normal patterns? Surveillance asks: Who is this person, and what else can I find out about them?

This distinction must be taught explicitly and repeatedly, because in the absence of clear instruction, officers default to their existing habits. Patrol officers are trained to investigate crimes, and investigation often involves gathering information about specific people. ILP reporting requires a different cognitive frame: gathering information about activities that may or may not be connected to crime, without presuming individual culpability. The shift is subtle but essential. An officer who cannot articulate it will either avoid reporting altogether—fearing civil liberties violations—or will report in a way that invites them.

Civil liberties protections are not an obstacle to intelligence-led policing; they are its foundation. When officers understand exactly what they should and should not report, they report with confidence. When communities see that law enforcement is documenting behaviors rather than identities, trust remains intact. A well-designed ILP training program devotes significant time to what not to report: religious practice, political speech, lawful association, immigration status unrelated to criminal activity, and protected First Amendment conduct. These are no exceptions to the reporting obligation; they are boundaries that define the obligation's shape.

The pocket card or field guide described later in this book can reinforce the distinction at the moment of decision, but the underlying mindset must be internalized before the card is ever consulted. An officer who fundamentally understands that their role is to report the "what," not the "who," will rarely need to consult a checklist to make the right call. The reporting-vs.-surveillance framework, once absorbed, becomes a self-correcting mechanism: it tells the officer when to report, when to document, and when to simply observe without recording.

Administrators and supervisors reinforce this framework through the questions they ask. An officer who submits a report describing an individual's ethnicity but not their behavior has missed the point—and the supervisor who reviews that report should say so, not as a reprimand but as a teaching moment. Over time, the agency's collective understanding sharpens, and the boundary between reporting and surveillance becomes not a source of anxiety but a point of professional pride. Officers who can articulate why their reporting respects civil liberties are officers who have truly understood the ILP mission.

Why Pattern Recognition Matters at the Patrol Level

Pattern recognition sounds like an analyst's skill, something that happens at a desk, with software, after multiple reports have been aggregated. But pattern recognition begins on the street, in the moment an officer notices that something is slightly off. A patrol officer who has worked in the same sector for three years knows the baseline: which cars park on which streets overnight, which businesses receive deliveries at odd hours, which faces belong and which ones don't. This knowledge is unconscious and deeply personal; it rarely makes it into a report because officers are not trained to think of their familiarity as data. Yet it is precisely this familiarity that makes pattern recognition possible at the patrol level.

The challenge is converting implicit knowledge into explicit reporting. An officer who notices the same rental truck outside a chemical supply company three times in a week may file that observation away as curious but unimportant. What the officer doesn't know—and cannot know—is that two officers in adjacent jurisdictions have noticed similar rental trucks near different chemical suppliers, and a fusion center analyst has flagged a national trend in precursor chemical theft for explosive manufacturing. The officer's single observation is a dot; the fusion center's capacity is to connect the dots. But the dots must be supplied, and that requires officers to trust that their seemingly minor observations might be significant.

Teaching pattern recognition to patrol officers doesn't mean teaching them to analyze; it means teaching them to notice with purpose. A simple shift in briefing language can prime this awareness: instead of telling officers to "be observant," a sergeant can provide specific indicators tied to current regional intelligence. "We've had reports of individuals asking unusual questions about bridge access and load limits in the tri-county area. If you see anyone photographing infrastructure from non-public vantage points, document the vehicle and the behavior and submit it." This instruction is concrete, constrained, and directly connected to a pattern—and it transforms the officer's patrol into a targeted information-gathering activity without adding a single minute to the shift.

The fusion center analyst who receives these reports experiences a different version of pattern recognition: the aggregation effect. A single report of someone photographing a bridge is noise; six reports of similar behavior at six bridges across three counties are a signal. But the signal emerges only if all six officers report, and they will only report if they understand that their individual observation, which may feel trivial—could be the piece that completes the puzzle. This understanding cannot be assumed; it must be communicated through examples, case studies, and feedback loops that show officers how aggregation works in practice.

One effective teaching tool is the retrospective case walkthrough. An instructor presents a real incident—a prevented attack, a disrupted smuggling operation—and traces it backward from the fusion center's analysis to the original patrol observations that launched the investigation. Officers see, often for the first time that the analyst's sophisticated threat picture was built from dozens of small, unremarkable reports submitted by officers just like them. The lesson is visceral: pattern recognition at the patrol level means knowing that no observation is too small to matter, because its significance depends on the observations of officers you have never met, in jurisdictions you have never patrolled.

Over time, officers who internalize this lesson begin to report more consistently and with greater specificity. They learn to include the details analysts need—time, location, vehicle description, observed behavior, and any contextual anomalies—without being reminded. The habit becomes professional instinct, and professional instinct, multiplied across a department and a region, becomes the foundation of a functioning intelligence system.

The Administrator's Role in Embedding ILP into Agency Culture

ILP cannot succeed as a specialized program housed in a single unit or driven by a single motivated supervisor. It must become part of the agency's operational culture, woven into hiring, training, supervision, evaluation, and daily practice. This transformation doesn't happen organically; it requires administrators to make deliberate, sustained choices that signal, in both large and small ways, that intelligence-led policing is not an add-on but an expectation.

The first signal is resource allocation. When an agency creates a dedicated intelligence officer position, assigns personnel to fusion center liaison duties, or funds attendance at regional intelligence conferences, it communicates that ILP is a priority worthy of investment. When an agency declines to do these things while issuing memos urging officers to "share information," it communicates the opposite. Officers are adept at reading the gap between rhetoric and resources; the gap tells them how seriously to take the message. Administrators who are serious about ILP must be willing to spend money, assign personnel, and protect those personnel from being pulled away to fill patrol shortages the moment staffing gets tight.

The second signal is performance evaluation. If an officer's annual review covers arrest numbers, traffic stops, and response times but never mentions intelligence reporting, the officer learns that intelligence reporting doesn't count. If, conversely, the evaluation includes a section on contributions to information sharing, not by volume of reports but by quality and consistency—the officer learns that this work matters. The measurement challenges around quality metrics are real and addressed elsewhere in this book, but the principle is straightforward: what gets evaluated gets done, and what gets ignored gets abandoned.

The third signal is supervisory reinforcement. Patrol sergeants are the bridge between administrative intent and street-level practice. If supervisors dismiss intelligence reporting as paperwork, officers will follow suit. If supervisors review suspicious activity reports with the same attention they give to arrest reports, officers will elevate the quality of their submissions. Administrators must therefore train supervisors not just in the mechanics of ILP but in the leadership behaviors that normalize it: asking about intelligence during shift briefings, debriefing officers after unusual encounters, and publicly recognizing officers whose reports contributed to a successful outcome.

The fourth signal, and perhaps the most powerful over time, is storytelling. Every agency has its lore—the big arrests, the near-misses, the cases that define careers. When administrators consistently highlight ILP success stories as part of that lore, they reshape the agency's understanding of what good police work looks like. The officer who stopped a vehicle for a traffic violation and filed a suspicious activity report that helped disrupt a weapons trafficking ring should be celebrated as much as the officer who made a high-profile felony arrest. The stories administrators choose to tell are the stories that officers aspire to live.

Embedding ILP also means planning for continuity. Administrators retire, transfer, or promote; intelligence officers move on. An agency that depends on a single champion to sustain its ILP culture will lose that culture when the champion leaves. Sustainable ILP requires institutionalization: written policies, standing training requirements, designated positions, and documented procedures that outlast any individual. The administrator who builds this infrastructure builds something that will serve the agency—and the public—long after their own career has ended.

Chapter 3: The Method – Practical Tools for Teaching ILP and Fusion Center Integration

The Training Sergeant's Dilemma

Sergeant Brutus had been handed another curriculum binder. At 50, with twenty-five years on the job and a dozen training initiatives behind him, he'd learned to recognize the look of a program destined for the shelf. The binder's spine was crisp, its tabs color-coded—fusion center awareness, suspicious activity reporting, intelligence cycle overview. Brutus flipped through it once, then set it on the corner of his desk where it stayed for three weeks. It wasn't that he disagreed with the content. It was that he'd seen this before: well-intentioned mandates delivered as information dumps, absorbed by no one, changing nothing. The disconnect Brutus felt wasn't about relevance, it was about translation. The material assumed officers already grasped why fusion centers mattered. But Brutus's experience told him that assumption was the whole problem.

Brutus's frustration captures a reality that training coordinators face nationwide. Policy directives arrive from state and federal partners, often rich in strategic language but thin on practical application for the patrol shift. The gap between what fusion centers need and what officers understand isn't a mystery, it's a curriculum design failure. And Brutus, like many educators in law enforcement, wasn't given a method; he was given a mandate. What follows in this chapter is the method he and others need: concrete tools for building training modules, exercises, and support materials that translate fusion center integration into a patrol officer's working vocabulary. The goal isn't simply awareness. It's operational fluency—officers who leave training not just knowing something about fusion centers but knowing what to do, what to report, and why it matters.

Building the Training Module: From Academy to In-Service

A training module that works begins with a single question: What should an officer be able to do differently after completing it? Too often, fusion center education starts and ends with a PowerPoint overview—what a fusion center is, how many there are, and which databases they access. That approach produces familiarity, not capability. The module must instead be built around behavioral outcomes. For recruits in the academy, the outcome is foundational: identify a suspicious activity indicator during a scenario and articulate why it warrants reporting. For in-service officers, the outcome deepens: connect observations across multiple calls to recognize a potential pattern, then document it in a format a fusion center analyst can actually use. These are different muscles, and the training must deliberately build each one.

The structure I've found most effective unfolds in three phases. Phase one is context: a brief, plain-language primer on how fusion centers receive and use information—not the org chart, but the workflow. Officers need to see the path their report will travel from their field notes to a desk officer's review to an analyst's mapping against other regional reports. Phase two is identification: scenario-based exercises where officers practice distinguishing between innocuous behavior and behavioral clusters that warrant reporting. Phase three is production: guided practice in writing a concise, factual intelligence report stripped of conclusions or assumptions. Each phase builds on the last, and together they create a graduating officer who doesn't just understand fusion centers, they can feed them.

For academy instructors, this means carving out dedicated hours, not tacking fusion center content onto a broader homeland security lecture. Four to six hours across a basic academy curriculum is realistic, with two hours in the first block and two to four later as scenarios grow more complex. For in-service, a half-day module every two years keeps the framework current. The key is sequence: recruits must practice reporting before they ever take a patrol shift, and veterans must refresh the skill before complacency sets in. The module isn't a one-time inoculation. It's a recurring discipline, and the schedule should reflect that.

The Signal vs. Noise Exercise

The most powerful training tool I've seen is also the simplest in design. It's called the Signal vs. Noise exercise, and it solves the problem of abstraction. Officers don't need theory; they need practice separating what matters from what isn't in the stream of daily contact. The exercise starts with a stack of twenty short field encounter cards. Each card describes a real-world patrol observation: a man photographing a bridge's support structure, a tenant reporting a neighbor's strange chemical smell, a business owner asking about their building's blueprints at city hall, a teenager flying a drone near a power substation, a delivery truck idling behind a closed shopping center at 2 a.m. Some are clearly benign. Some are clearly concerned. Most sit in the gray zone that officers navigate.

Participants work in pairs, sorting the twenty cards into two piles—Signal and Noise—and then defending their choices. What happens next is where the learning takes hold. The instructor reveals that three cards, drawn from real fusion center case files, were part of a larger pattern that contributed to a disrupted plot: the bridge photographs, the chemical smell, and the delivery truck were reported by three different officers in three different jurisdictions over ten days. None saw the connection alone. But when all three Signals arrived at a fusion center, an analyst linked them. The exercise isn't about getting the right answer. It's about feeling the moment when an isolated observation transforms into something larger—and realizing that the officer's job isn't to decide what matters. It's to report clearly so someone else can do so.

The debrief that follows should last as long as the sorting exercise itself. Facilitators guide officers through a set of questions, such as: What made you hesitate on the gray-zone cards? What would have helped you decide faster? Did you worry about appearing paranoid or like you were profiling? Those discussions surface the cultural and psychological barriers that no policy memo ever touches. The exercise makes visible the internal calculus officers perform on every call and gives instructors a direct path to reshaping that calculus. One session won't transform a skeptic, but repeated across an in-service cycle, it rewires the habit of dismissal.

The Fusion Center Field Guide: A Pocket Reference That Works

Training fades. Even the best module can't defeat the erosion of memory under stress, fatigue, and the competing priorities of a patrol shift. That's why every officer who completes ILP and fusion center training should leave with a physical artifact: a pocket field guide no larger than a departmental call card. This isn't a booklet. It's a single double-sided, laminated card that fits behind a badge or inside a uniform pocket. One side lists behavioral indicators organized not by threat category but by the patrol officer's natural workflow—Traffic Stops, Building Checks, Citizen Contacts, Suspicious Vehicle Observations. Under each heading, five to seven specific, observable actions: A vehicle with mismatched or obscured temporary plates; An individual filming security camera placement rather than landmarks; A tenant asking unusual questions about building evacuation procedures.

The reverse side contains the reporting template. It's starkly simple: Date, Time, Location, Subject Description, Observed Behavior, Vehicle or Property Information, and—critically—a single box labeled Why This Mattered to You. That last field isn't for analysts; it's for the officer. It captures the gut-level concern that prompted the report, the thing that felt off, written in plain words. Analysts later decode that field against threat databases, but its real function is to validate the officer's judgment. So much of the reporting gap comes from officers talking themselves out of their own instincts. The field guide gives that instinct a legitimate place on the page, making the report feel less like a bureaucratic form and more like professional communication.

The guide must be co-designed with patrol officers, not handed down by an administrator working alone. When a sergeant finally sat down with five patrol deputies and asked what they'd reference on a call, they cut the original 24 indicators down to 14 and rewrote half the language. They swapped "suspicious" for "unusual for this location at this time." They added a reminder line at the bottom: If you'd mention it to your partner, mention it here. That kind of ownership transforms the card from a mandate into a tool. It becomes something officers keep, not something they lose in a drawer.

The Administrator's Playbook: Embedding ILP in Agency Culture

Training alone has a self-life. Culture preserves it. An administrator's job isn't to teach the module—that's the trainer's role—but to build the structures that make the module's lessons stick. That work begins before training and continues long after. Three structural changes matter most: shift briefings, performance evaluations, and reward systems. Each is a level that can reinforce intelligence-led policing or quietly undermine it.

Shift briefings are the most underused asset in an agency's ILP effort. Ten minutes at the start of a patrol shift can convert abstract training into daily practice. The format is simple: a supervisor reads a brief intelligence summary—two or three recent fusion center bulletins relevant to the jurisdiction—and then asks a single question: What might you see tonight that connects to this? The question isn't rhetorical. It forces officers to prime their attention before they ever key the ignition. Over weeks, the priming becomes automatic. Officers start their shifts with their own observations, asking whether a particular vehicle or pattern has appeared in recent bulletins. The briefing shifts from a top-down broadcast into a conversation, and the conversation is evidence that the culture is changing.

Performance evaluations must follow. If an agency's evaluation rubric measures only traditional metrics—arrests, citations, response times—ILP participation becomes invisible, and invisible priorities die. Administrators need to add one weighted criterion: intelligence contribution. This isn't a quota system. It's a qualitative assessment by the officer's supervisor, documented quarterly: Did the officer submit any suspicious activity reports that demonstrated attention to detail? Did they reference fusion center bulletins during follow-up investigations? Did they contribute to shift discussions about pattern recognition? A simple three-point scale—Consistent, Developing, Not Observed—is enough. The goal isn't to quantify intelligence like a traffic stop tally; it's to signal that the agency sees and values the behavior.

Reward systems seal the change. When an officer's report contributes to a fusion center product that leads to an interdiction or disruption, that officer's name should appear in a commendation—not buried in a file but read aloud at a briefing or posted on a department-wide message. Some agencies have created an Intelligence Contribution Letter program: a formal acknowledgment, signed by the chief and copied to the fusion center director, placed in the officer's personnel file. The letter costs nothing. But it tells every officer in the agency that feeding the fusion center isn't extra work. It's recognized work. And recognition is the currency of cultural change.

Leveraging Existing Tools: eGuardian, LEEP, and the Patrol Workflow

No administrator wants to add a new login, a new database, or a new software burden to an already strained patrol operation. One of the fastest ways to kill ILP adoption is to present it as a separate system that requires officers to enter data twice at the end of a twelve-hour shift. The method must work with existing tools, not against them. Fortunately, the federal infrastructure already in place—eGuardian, the FBI's suspicious activity reporting platform, and LEEP, the Law Enforcement Enterprise Portal—can be integrated into patrol workflows if the integration is designed from the officer's perspective rather than the analyst's.

eGuardian is the backbone of nationwide suspicious activity reporting, but most patrol officers have never opened it. The reason isn't access—credentials are available through agency administrators. The reason is workflow fit. eGuardian is a database, not a reporting form, and officers need a bridge between them. The most effective bridge I've seen is a single-page agency form that mirrors the field guide template described earlier: observations, descriptors, context, and the officer's gut-check box. That form lives on the patrol car's mobile data terminal as a fillable PDF or a short web form. At the end of the shift, the officer opens the form, spends four minutes completing it, and submits it to their supervisor. The supervisor reviews it, then forwards it to a designated agency liaison who enters the data into eGuardian. The officer never touches eGuardian directly. Their interface is the field guide and the form. The fusion center's interface is eGuardian. The workflow respects both.

LEEP offers a different value: access to intelligence products that patrol officers can actually use. Through LEEP, officers can retrieve regional threat assessments, officer safety bulletins, and unclassified fusion center summaries relevant to their beat. The problem is that LEEP requires proactive logins, and most patrol officers don't know what to look for or when to look. The solution is to push LEEP content into the shift briefing rather than expecting officers to pull it. A designated intelligence officer—often a detective or a sergeant with fusion center liaison duties—monitors LEEP weekly, extracts two or three items relevant to current patrol operations, and distills them into the briefing format described above. The agency becomes a curated intelligence feed, and the patrol officer receives actionable information without ever having to navigate a federal portal. The complexity stays behind the scenes. The officer simply arrives at work better informed than they were yesterday.

The principle is consistent: the technology should serve the patrol officer's cognitive load, not increase it. Every additional click, login, or search query is a friction point where intelligence sharing can fail. The administrator's role is to clear those friction points, designing a system where the right information reaches the right officer at the right time—with the fewest possible steps in between.

Chapter 4: Recovery – When the System Breaks Down

The "False Positive" Problem

For the sake of anonymity, Bob hadn't expected the call. As chief of a small-town department, he was used to handling complaints—noise disputes, property-line arguments, and the occasional accusation of officer misconduct. But this was different. A week earlier, one of his patrol officers had submitted a suspicious activity report after seeing a man photographing a water treatment facility from a public road. The report went to the regional fusion center. Three days later, federal agents interviewed the man at his home. He turned out to be a civil engineer documenting infrastructure for a graduate thesis. Now a city council member was on the phone, demanding to know why her department was surveilling college students.

It's the scenario no one wants to discuss during the rollout of an intelligence-led policing program. You train officers to recognize indicators. You teach them that small signals matter. Then one of those signals turns out to be nothing—and the backlash lands squarely on the agency that did exactly what it was asked to do. The report wasn't malicious. It wasn't sloppy. The officer saw a behavior that matched a known pre-operational indicator, documented it, and forwarded it. But the outcome wasn't that the attack was prevented. It was an embarrassed student, an angry councilperson, and a department suddenly on the defensive.

This is the false positive problem, and it can undo months of careful work. When a report leads to an uncomfortable outcome, the instinct—for both officers and their supervisors—is to pull back. Submit fewer reports. Apply a higher threshold before flagging anything. The logic feels protective: if we only report the clearest threats, we reduce the risk of another embarrassing mistake. But the fusion center can't function on certainty. It needs the uncertain signals, the photos, the odd questions, the vehicles that don't quite fit—because those are the pieces that, combined with other fragments from other jurisdictions, form a recognizable picture.

The correction cannot stop reporting. The correction must be to understand what a false positive actually represents. In the intelligence cycle, a false positive isn't a failure—it's an indication that the system is sensitive enough to catch the real signals when they appear. Every screening process generates some number of false alarms. Medical tests do it. Fire alarms do it. The alternative is a system calibrated so narrowly that it misses the genuine threat. For fusion center reporting, that narrow calibration means an officer who hesitates to report the next suspicious photograph—the one that might not be a thesis project.

The response to a false positive has to be clear, consistent, and integrated into the training curriculum before the incident occurs. Agencies should prepare a script for community questions: what the report was, why it was made, how it was assessed, and what the outcome revealed. The officer who made the report should have heard from leadership that the action was correct, even if the result was benign. The focus stays on the process, not the outcome. An officer can control whether they recognize an indicator and report it competently; they can't control whether the subject turns out to be an engineer or a genuine threat. That distinction needs to be taught, reinforced, and modeled by supervisors.

The false positive also presents a curriculum opportunity—a ready-made case study for the next training session. Strip the identifying details, present the facts, and walk officers through the analysis. What did the officer observe? Which indicators were present? Why did the behavior match the reporting criteria? Then turn the conversation toward the aftermath—how the department handled it, what the officer felt, and why the system still worked as designed. Making the false positive part of the learning cycle removes its power to intimidate. An analyzed mistake becomes a teaching tool; an unexamined mistake becomes a reason to disengage.

There is one more dimension to this problem that instructors must address directly with their students: the emotional residue of being wrong in public. An officer who submits a report that triggers a federal response and then generates community outrage isn't just processing a policy issue. They're carrying the weight of having embarrassed their department, inconvenienced a citizen, and perhaps drawn media attention. That weight is real, and if it goes unaddressed, it calcifies into a personal policy: never again. A good curriculum makes space for that conversation, acknowledging that the desire to protect oneself from future scrutiny is natural, but that the mission requires a different response.

When Leadership Says No

Sometimes the resistance isn't at the street level. It's in the briefing room where the shift commander questions whether fusion center reporting is a productive use of patrol time. It's in the budget meeting where the chief weighs whether to send an officer to a regional intelligence conference. It's in the hallway conversation where a senior administrator says, flatly, "That's not what we do here." When leadership resists intelligence-led policing, the frontline officers take notes. They learn quickly which activities their supervisors value and which will earn them a side-glance. No amount of classroom training can overcome the signal sent by a lieutenant who dismisses a suspicious activity report as paranoid paperwork.

Administrative resistance takes several recognizable forms. The most common is the resource argument: we don't have the personnel, the funding, or the time to participate in fusion center programs. Sometimes this is genuine—a small agency with fifteen sworn officers genuinely cannot staff a liaison position. But often it's a prioritization choice dressed as a capacity problem. The same department that can't spare anyone for intelligence coordination manages to field a full-time D.A.R.E. officer, a school resource officer, and a task force representative for auto theft. The question isn't whether resources exist; it's what the agency deems important enough to allocate resources to.

Another form of resistance is jurisdictional skepticism. Some administrators view fusion centers as federal overreach, an intrusion into local policing decisions by agencies they don't trust and didn't elect. This perspective can run deep, particularly in regions where federal law enforcement has historically had a tense relationship with local departments. An administrator who believes the fusion center exists to collect information on their community rather than protect it will never fully cooperate—and that posture trickles down to every officer in the agency. Countering this requires more than policy arguments; it demands relationship-building between fusion center analysts and skeptical chiefs, demonstrating through repeated interaction that the partnership is mutual, not extractive.

The most challenging form of resistance arises from past failure. An administrator who participated in fusion center reporting years ago, only to see reports go unanswered or ignored intelligence requests, has learned a lesson the hard way: effort without feedback feels pointless. This is the quiet failure described earlier in this book, and its damage extends beyond the original incident. It conditions leadership to expect disappointment, to protect their officers from a system that doesn't seem to listen. When a new training initiative arrives promising better integration, that administrator isn't hostile—they're skeptical, and their skepticism is earned.

Addressing administrative resistance requires a different approach than addressing officer-level gaps. Administrators need evidence that the system works, presented in terms that matter to them: case studies showing how local reports led to actionable intelligence, data showing how fusion center participation improved investigative outcomes, and testimonials from peer agencies that overcame similar doubts. They also need a clear picture of what participation costs—an honest accounting of the time, training, and administrative burden, not a sanitized version that omits the friction points. An administrator who senses that they're being sold an easy solution will reinforce their defenses; one who's given the unvarnished reality can make an informed choice.

For the criminal justice educator, this topic belongs in the curriculum, not as a footnote but as a core competency. Students preparing for law enforcement careers need to understand that they may enter agencies where intelligence sharing isn't valued, and they need a mental framework for operating in such an environment. They should learn to document their reports regardless of supervisory reception, to build informal relationships with fusion center contacts through training events and regional meetings, and to recognize that institutional change often moves at a pace that frustrates a single career. The goal isn't to teach students to defy their chain of command; it's to teach them that persistent, quiet professionalism can incrementally shift an agency's culture.

Civil Liberties Complaints

The Great Tasting water treatment facility incident didn't end with the councilperson's phone call. Two days later, the local newspaper ran a story under the headline "Local Police Feed Federal Database with Innocent Man's Activities." The article quoted a privacy advocate who described the fusion center system as "domestic surveillance without oversight," and the student at the center of the story gave a television interview in which they said they felt "targeted for being curious about infrastructure." By the end of the week, the Great Tasting Water department had received forty-seven emails demanding an explanation, a formal records request for all suspicious activity reports filed in the prior year, and a visit from an ACLU attorney asking pointed questions about training protocols and audit procedures.

Civil liberties complaints are not hypothetical. They happen, and when they do, they arrive with legal, political, and reputational force. A department that has never thought through its response will find itself improvising under pressure—a position that almost always produces poor outcomes. The officer who made the original report gets isolated and defensive. The chief scrambles to explain a process she may not fully understand herself. The fusion center, bound by its own policies, may offer limited public assistance. And the community, watching all of this unfold, concludes that the system either violated someone's rights or lacks the transparency to prove it didn't.

The best defense against a civil liberties complaint is the one prepared long before the complaint arrives. Every agency participating in fusion center reporting should maintain a clear, publicly accessible policy that explains what types of behavior trigger a report, what information is included, what is explicitly excluded (political affiliation, religious practice, protected speech), and how the agency reviews reports for compliance. This policy serves multiple functions: it demonstrates good faith to oversight organizations, it gives officers a standard to follow, and it provides an immediate answer when the media calls. A department that can hand a reporter its written policy within ten minutes of a crisis breaking is in a fundamentally different position than one that asks for time to craft a statement.

The scenario also demands a curriculum response. In-service officers and criminal justice students need to practice navigating a civil liberties complaint in a controlled setting before they face one in their careers. A well-designed classroom exercise presents facts about a water treatment facility, divides students into roles—chief, reporting officer, journalist, civil liberties attorney, city council member—and walks through a simulated public meeting. The exercise forces students to articulate the distinction between reporting and surveillance, to explain why probabilistic intelligence gathering differs from individualized suspicion, and to acknowledge the real tension between security and privacy without dismissing either value. These aren't abstract debates; they're the conversations that occur in city halls and newspaper columns when a report becomes public.

The instructor's role in this exercise is not to resolve the tension. Students often want a clean answer: tell us whether the officer was right or wrong. But the real lesson is that intelligence-led policing operates in the space between certainty and ignorance, and that space will always generate friction. The officer was right to report the behavior—it matched established indicators, and failing to report would have been a missed opportunity if the subject had indeed been a threat. The officer was also operating within a system that, by design, produced a false positive. Neither of those statements cancels the other. Learning to hold both truths simultaneously—the accuracy of the process and the discomfort of the outcome—is what distinguishes a professional officer from one who either abandons reporting or defends it uncritically.

The civil liberties dimension also connects to something larger that should appear in every training module: the fusion center system's legitimacy depends on public trust, and public trust depends on demonstrated restraint. Every officer who files a report shapes that trust for better or worse. A sloppy report that includes irrelevant personal details damages the system far more than a missed indicator would. A report that carefully documents only the specific, articulable behaviors that triggered concerns such as photography of restricted infrastructure, use of binoculars near a sensitive location, and repeated visits at unusual hours—protects both the subject's rights and the system's credibility. The curriculum must teach that precision in reporting is not a bureaucratic nicety; it's a safeguard of civil liberties.

The After-Action Review

Not every failure is as visible as a newspaper story. Some failures are quieter—the missed opportunity, the delayed response, the piece of information that was reported but sat unread in an inbox until the window for action closed. These are the breakdowns that don't generate complaints because no one outside the system ever knows they happened. But inside the system, they erode confidence in the intelligence cycle, and they teach officers a corrosive lesson: your reports don't matter. The after-action review is the primary tool for interrupting that lesson and converting a breakdown into a corrective.

A properly structured after-action review does not assign blame. It assigns a process. The question isn't who failed but where the system failed—and systems fail at predictable points. A report sat in a queue because the analyst was overloaded. An indicator was dismissed because the receiving agency lacked the context to recognize its significance. A response was delayed because the fusion center lacked a clear escalation protocol for that specific threat type. These are structural problems, not personal failings, and the review should name them as such. An officer who learns that their report was received but mishandled learns something very different than an officer who simply never hears back at all.

The review also serves as a vital training function. When a breakdown occurs, the specific facts of the case—sanitized for privacy—become the raw material for the next curriculum update. Officers can study the timeline: when the initial observation was made, when the report was filed, where the delay occurred, and what might have been different if the information had moved faster. These retrospectives are far more effective than hypothetical scenarios because they carry the weight of consequence; something actually happened, or almost happened, and the analysis matters because the outcome was real. The curriculum should institutionalize this cycle, ensuring that every significant breakdown in an agency's intelligence process feeds back into the training materials within six months.

One of the most challenging scenarios in an after-action review is an unreported near miss. A patrol officer sees something concerning—a rented truck parked near a federal building, a chemical odor from a storage unit, a set of questions at a hardware store that doesn't add up—and files it mentally but never on paper. Weeks later, an incident occurs elsewhere that matches the pattern. The officer realizes, with a sinking feeling, that their observation might have contributed to a broader awareness if they had shared it. The review of this kind of failure must be handled with exceptional care. The officer already carries the weight of the missed opportunity; a review that adds shame or discipline only reinforces the original hesitation.

The more productive approach uses the near-miss as a teaching moment for the entire agency, without identifying the officer involved. A case study is constructed from the facts: the indicators present, the officer's thought process, the reasons reporting didn't occur—lack of confidence, uncertainty about the threshold, fear of looking foolish. The training session then walks through the same scenario and asks officers to identify when and how a report should have been made, what specific language the report should have used, and what the fusion center might have done with the information. The goal is to normalize the reporting impulse so thoroughly that the next officer in the same situation doesn't hesitate.

Finally, the after-action review must produce a specific, documented change. If the breakdown occurred because officers didn't know which indicators to watch, the training module is updated. If it occurred because the reporting system was cumbersome, the interface gets streamlined. If it occurred because the fusion center wasn't sharing analytic products back to the agency, the liaison relationship gets renegotiated. A review that generates only discussion and no action is, in itself, a failure. Officers need to see that when problems are identified, solutions follow. That visibility is what rebuilds the trust that a breakdown erodes.

Restoring Trust After a Breakdown

Trust is easier to lose than to rebuild, and in the context of intelligence sharing, it fractures along multiple fault lines simultaneously. A breakdown can damage trust between the patrol officer and the fusion center, between the agency and its community, between line personnel and their own leadership, and between the department and external oversight bodies. Repairing each of these relationships requires a different approach, but they all share a common starting point: the honest acknowledgment that something went wrong, without evasion. An agency that can't say "the process didn't work as intended, and here's what we're doing about it" will find that every subsequent communication is met with skepticism.

The first relationship to repair is the one between the officer and the system. An officer who filed a report that contributed to a problematic outcome—or who saw a colleague go through that experience—needs to hear from the fusion center directly, not through a memo, not through a training bulletin, but through a conversation, preferably with the analyst who handled the report or the center's law enforcement liaison. The conversation should explain what happened to the report after it left the officer's hands, what the review process revealed, and what structural changes are being implemented. Officers don't need to be shielded from bad news; they need to be treated as professionals who can understand complex systems when those systems are explained honestly.

Community trust requires a different kind of repair, one that goes beyond the single incident. A department facing a civil liberties controversy over a fusion center report can't simply resolve the case and declare trust restored. The community's concern is rarely about one report; it's about the pattern the report seems to represent. The department needs to demonstrate, over time, that its intelligence-sharing practices are bound, accountable, and transparent. This might mean publishing an annual summary of suspicious activity reports, how many were filed, what categories they fell into, how many resulted in further investigation, and how many were determined to be innocent activity. A department willing to share this data publicly signals confidence in its own processes; one that resists such transparency signals the opposite.

Trust between the patrol division and the administration requires a different set of actions. Line officers need to see that their leadership will defend appropriate reports even when those reports draw criticism. A chief who publicly explains why a particular observation met the reporting criteria, even while acknowledging the unfortunate outcome, sends a message that the officers in the field are supported. A chief who distances herself from the officer, or who implements blanket restrictions on reporting categories to avoid future complaints, sends a different message entirely—one that says protection flows up, not down. The curriculum for future supervisors should include case studies of both responses so that students entering leadership roles understand what's at stake.

Restoring trust with oversight bodies—civil liberties organizations, city councils, civilian review boards—requires a willingness to engage in good faith. These groups are not inherently hostile to intelligence-led policing; many of their members recognize that information sharing is a legitimate law enforcement function. What they resist is opacity. An agency that invites a privacy advocate to review its reporting policy and offers feedback, or that includes a civil liberties component in its training curriculum and publicizes that fact, demonstrates that security and rights can coexist. This engagement is not a concession; it's a strategic investment in the system's long-term viability. A fusion center that operates without public legitimacy is one controversy away from being defunded or defanged.

For the criminal justice educator, the topic of trust restoration belongs at the end of the recovery curriculum for a reason. It draws together all the other threads—the false positive, the resistant administrator, the civil liberties complaint, the after-action review—and asks students to see them as parts of a single, ongoing institutional challenge. Breakdowns are not aberrations in intelligence-led policing; they are predictable features of a system that generates probabilistic assessments in a public environment. The question isn't whether a breakdown will occur. The question is whether the agency has built the relationships and the processes to survive one when it does.

Chapter 5: Identity Shift – The Intelligence-Led Officer as a Career Standard

From Incidental Reporter to Proactive Collector

Joe had 31 years on the job, and a retirement date circled on his calendar. He didn't dislike fusion centers, but he simply didn't think about them. His patrol philosophy was built on answering calls, clearing them, and moving to the next. When a training sergeant handed him a pocket card listing indicators of suspicious activity, he stuffed it in his glove box and forgot about it. Six months later, Joe responded to a burglary at a chemical supply warehouse where the only items stolen were large quantities of acetone and hydrogen peroxide—precursors Joe recognized from an old arson investigation. He wrote the report. He cleared the call. He didn't flag it for intelligence review because no one had ever shown him that a burglary report could be a counterterrorism lead. The warehouse manager mentioned to a different officer two days later that a man had been photographing the loading dock the previous week. That detail went into a separate report and sat in the records system until an FBI agent requesting similar thefts in two neighboring states finally connected the dots three weeks later. Joe wasn't negligent; he was operating inside the identity he had been trained for his entire career: respond, document, clear, repeat.

This is the identity gap the entire fusion center system depends on closing. The shift from incidental reporter to proactive collector isn't about adding a task to an officer's shift, it's about rewiring what the officer believes their job actually includes. An incidental reporter notices something unusual and writes a report when a crime is obvious or a victim demands it. A proactive collector notices the same thing but recognizes that the information has value regardless of whether a penal code violation is immediately apparent. That recognition changes what the officer sees, what they document, and what they submit. A vehicle parked repeatedly at an overpass overlooking a rail yard isn't a crime. A tenant paying three months' rent in cash while receiving no mail isn't a crime. A customer asking detailed questions about the placement of store security cameras isn't a crime. In the incidental reporter's world, these events fade into the background noise of a shift. In the proactive collector's world, they rise to the level of something worth documenting and forwarding—not because the officer is certain something is wrong, but because the officer understands that uncertainty itself is information worth sharing.

This mental shift depends on a single conviction: the officer believes the fusion center will use the information well. Belief doesn't come from memos or policy directives. It comes from seeing the mechanism work—from receiving a follow-up call that says, "That detail you sent about the storage unit rental? It matched three other reports we didn't know were connected. Thank you." Without that feedback loop, proactive collection feels like throwing information into a void. With it, the behavior becomes self-reinforcing. One officer who receives meaningful acknowledgment will tell two others. Over time, the identity shifts from "I answer calls" to "I contribute to threat awareness." That second identity doesn't just change reporting volume; it changes how the officer listens during interviews, how they observe during traffic stops, and how they document seemingly minor details in their narrative reports.

The training modules described earlier in this book can teach the mechanics of what to report and how to do so. But identity change requires something those modules alone can't deliver: repeated experiences of agency. An officer has to feel that their observation made a difference—not once, but consistently enough that the behavior becomes part of their professional self-image. Agencies that succeed in this shift treat intelligence contributions the same way they treat arrests or case clearances: they name them, they count them, and they celebrate them. A shift briefing that includes "Officer Brutus's suspicious-activity report last Tuesday helped the fusion center link a pattern across three counties" does more identity-building work than ten hours of classroom instruction. The message is clear: this is what good police work looks like now.

There is a generational dimension here that agencies ignore at their peril. New recruits enter the academy with no fixed identity as patrol officers; they are malleable in ways that veterans like Joe are not. If the academy curriculum embeds intelligence collection into the core definition of patrol work—right alongside traffic enforcement, domestic violence response, and report writing—new officers will simply accept it as part of the job. They won't need to unlearn years of reactive policing habits. Veterans, by contrast, have decades of reinforced neural pathways that tell them good policing means closing calls quickly and moving on. Retraining them requires acknowledging that their existing identity isn't deficient, it's simply incomplete for the current threat environment. The most effective approach frames proactive collection not as a replacement for traditional patrol skills but as an extension of them: "You already know how to notice things that don't fit. We're going to add one step to that instinct—documenting and forwarding what you notice."

Joe eventually made the shift, though not because of a training module. A near-miss changed him. A federal alert about a planned attack on a regional power substation included details that matched something Joe had seen three months earlier: a van parked near a substation access road with a man using a camera on a tripod—not a smartphone, not a tourist snapshot, but a mounted camera aimed at the infrastructure. Joe had thought it was odd. He had mentioned it to his partner. He hadn't written a report because there was no crime. When he saw the alert, the blood drained from his face. He called the fusion center himself that afternoon, and the analyst who took his call treated his three-month-old observation like gold. That single interaction did more to shift Joe's identity than twenty years of policy changes could have. He became one of his agency's most reliable intelligence contributors in the final two years of his career, not because someone told him to, but because he finally understood the value of his observations.

For educators designing curricula, Joe's story contains a critical insight: identity shifts are triggered by felt consequences, not by information. Trainees need to experience the weight of a missed opportunity or the satisfaction of a contributed success—if not directly, then through scenarios vivid enough to generate the same emotional response. Case studies of near-misses, actual prevented attacks, and delayed intelligence connections serve as proxy experiences that begin the identity shift before the officer ever hits the street. The curriculum can't just teach what fusion centers do; it must make the learner feel what it's like to be the officer who connected the dots—or the officer who didn't.

The Fusion Center Liaison Officer Model

The gap between a fusion center's analytical capability and a patrol officer's daily reality is wide enough that information often falls into it. Someone needs to stand in that gap. The liaison officer model places a designated individual—or, in larger agencies, a small team—directly inside the patrol division to serve as the living bridge between street-level observations and the fusion center's analytical machinery. This isn't a full-time intelligence analyst position. It's a patrol officer or sergeant with additional training who retains regular duties but also carries the explicit responsibility of translating fusion center products into patrol-relevant language and translating patrol observations into intelligence-grade submissions. The model works because it solves the two largest barriers to information flow: the patrol officer doesn't know what the fusion center needs, and the fusion center doesn't know what the patrol officer is seeing. The liaison lives in both worlds.

For instance, Mary, a patrol sergeant in a mid-sized department, served as the fusion center liaison after her agency's previous attempts at intelligence integration had fizzled. She spent one day each month at the state fusion center, sitting with analysts and learning which patrol-level observations had proven valuable in past cases. She learned that analysts didn't need officers to determine what was suspicious—they needed raw, unfiltered observations: descriptions, license plates, timelines, and contextual details the officer might consider mundane. Mary brought that knowledge back to her shift briefings and translated it into language her officers could act on immediately: "If you see someone photographing infrastructure from an unusual angle, just write down the location, time, vehicle description, and what the person was doing. Don't decide whether it matters. Send it to me, and I'll forward it." Reporting in her squad increased eightfold within two months—not because the officers were doing anything different on patrol, but because Mary had removed the cognitive burden of determining relevance. The officers could observe and document; Mary made the threshold decision on whether the observation warranted a fusion center submission.

The liaison role also solves the feedback problem that undermines so many intelligence-sharing initiatives. As explored in Chapter 4, reporting behaviors collapse when officers feel their submissions disappear into a void. The liaison officer is perfectly positioned to close that loop. When Mary received acknowledgment from the fusion center that an officer's observation had contributed to a broader pattern analysis, she made that acknowledgment public during the next shift briefing—naming the officer, describing the observation, and explaining how it fit a larger picture. The effect was electric. Officers who had never considered themselves part of the intelligence apparatus suddenly saw their mundane patrol observations as valuable contributions to something larger than their beat. The liaison didn't just transmit information; she transmitted meaning. She gave the officers a reason to believe their extra effort mattered.

Implementing the liaison model requires administrators to make two specific decisions. First, the liaison must be given genuine authority to shape patrol reporting practices—not just a title and a laminated card. This means the liaison's recommendations about what to report and how to document it carry the weight of supervisory expectation. If a patrol officer ignores the liaison's guidance and a subsequent intelligence gap is identified, the failure should be treated as a performance issue, not shrugged off as optional. Second, the agency must protect the liaison's time. A liaison who is expected to absorb the role on top of a full patrol workload without any adjustment will burn out or, worse, treat the role as an afterthought. Even a modest reduction in call load—one fewer call per shift, one administrative day per month—signals that the agency takes the function seriously and gives the liaison the bandwidth to do the work well.

The liaison model also creates a natural pipeline for intelligence-minded officers to develop deeper expertise. Officers who serve as liaisons often become the agency's most knowledgeable personnel on threat indicators, fusion center capabilities, and information-sharing protocols. Some will pursue advanced training; others will rotate into full-time analytical roles. The existence of the liaison position signals to every patrol officer in the agency that intelligence work is not a separate career track reserved for federal agents and analysts but a natural progression within local law enforcement. That signaling effect does identity-shifting work across the entire department, not just for the individual liaison. It says, in effect: "The skills you develop here can lead somewhere."

Small agencies that can't dedicate a sworn officer to the liaison role have options. A regional liaison model—where several small departments share one liaison officer funded through a grant or interagency agreement—achieves the same bridge function without placing an unsustainable burden on any single agency. The shared liaison rotates through the participating departments, learns each agency's culture and reporting habits, and serves as the single point of contact for the regional fusion center. The model has the added benefit of standardizing reporting practices across multiple agencies, which makes the fusion center's analytical work more consistent and reliable. What matters is the function, not the staffing number: someone must own the responsibility of translating between the patrol officer's world and the analyst's world, or the gap described in Chapter 1 will persist regardless of how many training modules are delivered or how many policy memos are issued.

Measuring Success: Metrics Beyond Report Counts

Agencies love counting things. Arrests. Citations. Case clearances. When intelligence reporting becomes a stated priority, the natural bureaucratic instinct is to count reports—how many suspicious activity reports were submitted this month? How does that compare to last month? Are the numbers going up? This instinct is understandable and, left unchecked, destructive. The moment the report count becomes the primary metric, reporting quality degrades. Officers who are evaluated on volume will submit anything that might plausibly qualify, flooding the fusion center with noise, burning out analysts, and eroding the very trust the system depends on. The fusion center that receives 500 reports a month but finds only three actionable is worse off than the fusion center that receives 50 reports and finds 20 actionable—not only because the analytical burden is higher, but because the signal-to-noise ratio makes it harder to identify genuine threats. The metric that matters isn't the number of reports submitted. It's how many reports contributed to analytical products, investigative leads, or threat assessments that would not have existed otherwise.

Measuring contribution rather than volume requires a feedback loop from the fusion center back to the agency. The fusion center must be willing and able to tag submitted reports with outcome codes: "Contributed to an existing case," "Matched a pattern across jurisdictions," "Resulted in a new investigative lead," "Provided useful context but no immediate action," or "Insufficient detail to assess." These outcome codes, stripped of sensitive details, can be returned to the submitting agency and tracked over time. An officer who submits ten reports that generate five investigative leads is outperforming an officer who submits fifty reports that generate none—and the metric should reflect that. This approach also allows administrators to identify officers whose reports consistently add value and to study what they're doing differently. Are they documenting specific details that other officers miss? Are they focusing on particular categories of suspicious activity? The answers can inform training and shift-briefing content far more effectively than a generic exhortation to "report more."

There is a second metric that matters enormously and is seldom tracked: timeliness. An observation reported within an hour of the encounter has a fundamentally different value proposition than the same observation reported three days later—especially when the observation relates to pre-operational surveillance or attack planning. Fusion center analysts consistently report that the single greatest variable in whether a patrol submission contributes to a disruption effort is how quickly it arrives. Timeliness metrics—average time from observation to submission and the percentage of reports submitted within the same shift—should be tracked and incorporated into performance expectations. An officer who reliably submits high-quality reports before the end of the shift is contributing more to threat awareness than an officer who submits a higher volume but batches reports at the end of the week. Speed matters, and what gets measured gets improved.

The third dimension of measurement is harder to quantify but essential: the effect of intelligence contributions on the officer's own investigations and patrol effectiveness. Officers who habitually query fusion center databases before starting a shift—checking for recent threat assessments, suspicious activity reports in their patrol area, or analytical products relevant to local infrastructure—consistently report that the practice changes what they notice on patrol. An officer who knows from a fusion center bulletin that a specific type of cargo theft is trending in the region will pay different attention to the trucks in their patrol area than an officer who hasn't seen that bulletin. Measuring this effect requires surveying officers on whether intelligence products influenced their patrol decisions, investigative approaches, or officer-safety calculations. The surveys don't produce tidy numbers for the monthly report, but they capture the downstream value of intelligence integration in a way that simple report counts never will.

Agencies that get this right treat intelligence contributions the way they treat arrests: as professional achievements worth documenting, celebrating, and incorporating into promotion considerations. An officer seeking a specialty assignment or a promotion to sergeant should be able to point to a record of high-quality, timely intelligence contributions with the same pride they point to a record of felony arrests. When the agency's formal incentive structure aligns with the intelligence-sharing mission, the identity shift described earlier in this chapter accelerates. The officer doesn't have to choose between "doing my job" and "feeding the fusion center." The two become indistinguishable because the agency's measurement system treats them as the same thing.

The Generational Shift: Training New Recruits vs. Retraining Veterans

The officer who enters the academy in 2026 has never known a world where local law enforcement wasn't expected to contribute to national threat awareness. The post-9/11 information-sharing architecture is older than they are. Their baseline assumptions about policing include a role for intelligence, even if they can't articulate it clearly. The 55-year-old veteran with 30 years on the job entered policing in an era when the FBI handled terrorism, the DEA handled drugs, and the patrol officer handled calls for service. Those two officers inhabit the same agency, work the same shifts, and are subject to the same policies. But their starting points for understanding intelligence-led policing could not be more different. Any training strategy that treats them identically will fail one of them—and probably both.

New recruits arrive with a blank identity slate, which is both an opportunity and a risk. The opportunity is obvious: if the academy embeds intelligence collection into the foundational definition of patrol work, the recruit will accept it as naturally as they accept report writing or traffic enforcement. They won't need to be persuaded. They won't carry the institutional memory of an era when "intelligence" meant something separate and federal. The risk is subtler: recruits who are taught that every observation might be intelligence can develop a hyper-vigilance that produces exactly the overreporting problem described in Chapter 4. The academy curriculum must balance two messages simultaneously—"Your observations matter to national security" and "Most observations will not be intelligence, and that's normal." This balancing act is harder than it sounds. It requires instructors to teach discernment, not just enthusiasm, and to normalize the idea that submitting nothing on a quiet shift is not a failure.

The most effective academy approach integrates intelligence concepts into every existing block of instruction rather than isolating them in a standalone "fusion center awareness" module. When recruits learn traffic stops, they learn to document indicators that might be relevant to a fusion center analysis—not just citations and warnings. When they learn domestic violence response, they learn to recognize circumstances that might intersect with radicalization or weapons acquisition. When they learn report writing, they learn to include the specific details analysts need: exact times, license plates with state, physical descriptions that include clothing and distinguishing features, and context that explains why the officer found something notable. By the time the recruit graduates, intelligence awareness isn't an additional competency—it's woven into every competency they already possess.

Veteran retraining requires a fundamentally different approach. The veteran officer doesn't need to be taught from scratch; they need to be shown that the skills they already possess have an application they may not have recognized. The best retraining programs start with respect: "You've been noticing things that don't fit for 20 years. That instinct is exactly what intelligence-led policing depends on. What we're adding is a deliberate step to document and forward what your gut already flags." This framing avoids the defensiveness that arises when veterans feel they're being told their career's work is incomplete or outdated. It honors their experience while redirecting it toward a new purpose.

Experienced officers also need to hear from other experienced officers who have made the shift. A training module delivered by a 25-year veteran who describes, in plain language, how he nearly missed a critical piece of intelligence and what he changed afterward will land with far more weight than the same content delivered by an analyst or an administrator. Peer credibility is the currency of veteran retraining. Agencies serious about the identity shift should identify officers who have credibility with their veteran peers—officers respected for their street sense, their case clearance rates, their no-nonsense approach—and enlist them as ambassadors for the intelligence mission. Let the skeptic hear from someone who was also skeptical. Let the reluctant officer hear from someone who was also reluctant. The messenger matters at least as much as the message.

The generational gap also creates a mentorship opportunity that agencies rarely exploit. Pair a veteran officer with a recent academy graduate and give them a joint assignment: identify three observations during a shift that might warrant an intelligence submission and discuss whether and how to report them. The veteran brings pattern recognition refined by years of experience; the recruit brings the academy's framework for what constitutes a reportable indicator. Each learns from the other. The veteran sees the framework applied to real situations and begins to trust it; the recruit sees how experienced judgment filters and contextualizes the framework. Over time, the pairing produces officers at both career stages who are more sophisticated about intelligence than either would be alone. The mentorship also breaks down the "us versus them" dynamic that can develop between generations, replacing it with a shared investment in the agency's intelligence capability.

The Ripple Effect: Beyond Fusion Centers

The investment in shifting an officer's identity from reactive responder to proactive collector pays dividends far beyond the fusion center's analytical products. An officer who habitually documents detailed observations, queries databases for context, and thinks in terms of patterns rather than isolated incidents is a more effective criminal investigator, a more attentive community policing officer, and a safer officer on the street. The identity doesn't just activate when the officer sees something that might be terrorism-related; it shifts how the officer approaches every call, every contact, every report. The ripple effect transforms the agency's overall capability in ways that are easy to feel but hard to attribute to any single policy change.

Consider criminal investigations. Detectives routinely complain that patrol officers' initial reports lack the detail needed to identify suspects, establish timelines, or connect cases. The officer trained in intelligence collection writes a fundamentally different report than the officer trained only to document probable cause. The intelligence-minded officer includes vehicle descriptions with license plates, notes whether a witness seemed evasive or unusually knowledgeable, documents the presence of multiple cell phones or financial documents, and records contextual details about the scene that might connect the incident to other reported crimes. When a detective picks up that report three days later, the investigative starting point is dramatically stronger. The case moves faster. The clearance rate improves. None of this shows up in the fusion center's metrics, but it is a direct product of the same identity shift this chapter has described.

Community policing also offers benefits, though the connection is less obvious. Officers who see themselves as intelligence collectors tend to ask better questions during casual community contacts. They don't interrogate. They listen more attentively to the business owner who mentions that a new tenant in the strip mall is paying in cash and never opens during business hours. They follow up on the neighbor's offhand comment about a rental truck that appears every Thursday night and leaves before dawn. These conversations don't feel like intelligence gathering to the community member; they feel like a police officer who is genuinely interested in what's happening in the neighborhood. Trust builds. Information flows more freely. The community sees a police department that is present and attentive, not just responsive. The intelligence-collection function and the community-engagement function reinforce each other in a virtuous cycle, making both stronger.

Officer safety is the benefit that patrol officers feel most viscerally. An officer who queries fusion center databases before a shift and learns that a particular address has been associated with weapons stockpiling approaches that call differently than an officer who arrives with no context. An officer who knows from a regional bulletin that a specific gang is using a new tactic to ambush responding officers is more likely to recognize the setup and adjust their approach. Intelligence isn't just for analysts; it's a survival tool that gives officers information they can't get from their own experience or their shift briefing alone. When officers experience this benefit directly—when a piece of intelligence alerts them to a danger they wouldn't have anticipated—the identity shift accelerates. Self-preservation is a more powerful motivator than any policy.

Finally, the ripple effect reaches into recruitment and retention. The profession of policing is competing for talent in a difficult labor market. Agencies that can offer a career path that includes intelligence specialization, liaison roles, and meaningful participation in regional threat awareness have a recruiting message that generic "serve and protect" departments don't. Younger candidates who grew up in the information age are drawn to roles that feel sophisticated, connected to something larger than local calls for service, and intellectually engaging. The agency that treats intelligence as a core patrol function, not a specialized sideline, can attract and retain officers who would otherwise gravitate toward federal or analytical careers. The fusion center partnership, in other words, isn't just a public safety asset—it's a workforce asset that makes the department more competitive in the long run.

Conclusion

The Quiet Gap Revisited

This book opens with a question rarely asked directly: Do the people on the ground really understand what fusion centers are for? After examining the perceptions of administrators and practitioners, walking through the mechanics of intelligence-led policing, and laying out practical training tools, the answer comes into sharper focus. Understanding is patchy. It varies by agency, by shift, by individual officer. And where understanding thins out, the system does not announce its failure. It simply underperforms—quietly, gradually, without a single moment of blame.

That is the quiet gap. It is not a scandal. It is not a policy failure that makes headlines. It is the accumulated weight of small missed signals, reports that never get written, patterns that dissolve before anyone connects them. The fusion center model was built on a sound premise: that local officers are the eyes and ears of homeland security. But eyes and ears need a brain that knows what to look for. Without that, the sensory network is active but unguided.

What this book has attempted to do is not diagnose a catastrophe, but illuminate a condition. A condition in which good officers, doing their jobs conscientiously, simply do not have the conceptual framework to see their own role inside the intelligence cycle. They respond to calls. They write incident reports. They testify in court. But contributing to a fusion center's threat picture? That feels foreign—and feeling foreign, it slips down the priority list until it disappears altogether.

Yet the research and the practitioner accounts gathered here point toward something hopeful. This gap is not fixed. It is not a permanent feature of law enforcement culture. It exists because training has not kept pace with expectations. And training, as any educator knows, is a solvable problem. It requires curriculum design, institutional commitment, and a willingness to treat intelligence sharing not as an add-on but as a core competency—right alongside defensive tactics and constitutional law.

The patrol officer who can distinguish between a routine observation and a threat indicator is not a different breed of officer. They are simply an officer who has been taught what to pay attention to, how to document it, and why it matters beyond their own shift. That teaching is the through-line of every chapter that preceded this one. The problem was defined. The ILP mindset was framed. The methods were laid out. The recovery strategies were explored. And the identity shift was envisioned. What remains is the question of who will carry this forward.

The Educator as the Pivot Point

If the quiet gap is a training problem, then the people who design and deliver training are the pivot point. That means criminal justice professors, academy instructors, field training officers, and in-service coordinators. These are the professionals who shape what a new officer thinks the job actually is—not just what the policy manual says, but what the daily practice demands. When an instructor treats fusion center reporting as a footnote, the officer will treat it as optional. When a curriculum buries ILP in a single lecture during week twelve of the academy, the message is clear: this is not central.

Educators have a unique kind of leverage. They do not just transmit information; they establish what counts as professional competence. A recruit who can recite the elements of a burglary statute but cannot identify a suspicious activity indicator relevant to terrorism is half-trained for the world they will actually police. And the instructor who leaves that gap in place—whether from time constraints, institutional inertia, or their own unfamiliarity—has made a choice, even if unintentionally. The choice is to let the quiet gap persist into another generation of policing.

What would it look like if educators took ownership of this problem? It would start with a decision to treat ILP not as a specialty topic but as a thread woven through the entire curriculum. A lesson on traffic stops could include a five-minute segment on what indicators beyond the traffic violation itself might warrant a report. A scenario on domestic disturbance calls could end with a debrief question: "Was there anything here that a fusion center analyst might want to know?" Small integrations, repeated over months, compound. They shift the baseline of what a patrol officer considers worth noticing.

This does not require educators to become intelligence analysts themselves. It requires them to understand the system's architecture well enough to teach its entry points. That is a manageable ask. The resources already exist—threat liaison officers, fusion center liaison officers, online portals, field guides. What has been missing is the curricular will to place those resources in front of students and say, "This is part of your job, and here is why." The educator who makes that statement has closed a piece of the quiet gap for every officer who passes through their classroom.

Students absorb what the instructor signals as important. If the instructor signals that intelligence sharing is a bureaucratic abstraction, students will nod and forget. If the instructor signals that it is a professional obligation with real protective consequences, students will internalize it. The signal matters. And the signal is entirely within the educator's control.

Civil Liberties and the Intelligence-Led Officer

No discussion of fusion centers and intelligence sharing can conclude without addressing the tension that hovers over the entire enterprise: the relationship between proactive information collection and civil liberties. This tension is real. It has generated lawsuits, public backlash, and deep mistrust in some communities. An officer trained to notice and report suspicious patterns may, without careful guidance, drift into profiling based on constitutionally protected characteristics. That risk cannot be dismissed or minimized.

But the tension is not irresolvable. In fact, the ILP framework described throughout this book contains its own safeguards—if training emphasizes them. The distinction between reporting patterns and surveilling people is fundamental. A fusion center benefits from knowing that someone rented a cargo van using cash and a false address; it does not benefit from knowing that someone attends a particular mosque. The former is a behavioral indicator. The latter is a constitutionally protected activity. Training that conflates the two creates legal liability and community damage. Training that differentiates them creates both safety and trust.

The classroom is where this differentiation must be taught with precision. Scenario-based exercises, as suggested in the methods chapter, are particularly effective in this context. Students can be presented with ambiguous situations—a person taking photographs of a bridge, a neighbor reporting unusual chemical smells—and asked to identify what is reportable and what crosses into protected territory. The debrief is where the instructor draws a sharp line and where the future officer learns that intelligence-led policing and constitutional policing are not competitors. They are requirements that must coexist.

Administrators also play a role in this balance. Policies that define what constitutes reportable suspicious activity, require supervisory review before submission, and include clear prohibitions on racial or religious profiling create an institutional safety net. The field guide and training module suggested earlier in this book should include not just indicators of threat but indicators of overreach—what not to report, and why. Civil liberties protections are not an obstacle to intelligence sharing; they are a prerequisite for its legitimacy.

A community that trusts its police department will share information voluntarily. A community that fears its police department will hide it. The math is simple. Officers trained in both ILP and civil liberties are the bridge between these two outcomes. They collect what is necessary for threat awareness without sacrificing what is necessary for democratic policing. The fusion center system cannot function in the long term without that bridge. And the bridge is built first in the classroom, reinforced in field training, and maintained through administrative accountability.

A Practical Invitation

The chapters of this book have moved from problem to principle, from recovery method, and finally to identity. Each layer builds on the one before it, but none of them are theoretical. They are drawn from the lived experience of administrators and practitioners who navigate the fusion center system every day—sometimes with clarity, sometimes with confusion. The confusion is not a character flaw. It is a predictable outcome of asking agencies to adopt a new paradigm without fully equipping their people to understand it. That can change.

The invitation here is not to a grand restructuring of homeland security policy. It is a focused, achievable shift in how law enforcement training addresses intelligence sharing. An academy curriculum that includes a robust fusion center module. An in-service program that refreshes pattern recognition skills. A field training officer who models reporting as casually as they model officer safety. A police chief who asks not just about crime stats but about intelligence contributions: these are small moves, but they aggregate across an agency, and across the profession, into a culture that closes the quiet gap.

For the criminal justice professor, the invitation is to assign this book—not as the final word, but as a starting point for classroom discussion. Let students wrestle with the scenarios. Let them debate the civil liberties questions. Let them imagine themselves as the officer who saw something, wrote it up, and, three weeks later, learned that their report was part of a broader threat picture. That moment of realization, even in a hypothetical classroom exercise, plants a seed. The seed is this: my observations matter, and I am part of a system larger than my patrol district.

For the academy instructor, the invitation is to audit the current curriculum and ask a blunt question: where does fusion center integration actually appear, and is that placement enough? If the answer is a single PowerPoint slide in a homeland security overview, the curriculum is not doing its job. The methods outlined in this book—the signal-versus-noise exercise, the field guide, the scenario debriefs—are ready to be adapted. They require no special technology. They require a shift in instructional priority. That shift is free, and its payoff is officers who leave the academy knowing what their fusion center expects of them.

The work of closing the quiet gap is slow, incremental, and largely invisible. It does not produce press conferences. It does not yield dramatic statistics. But it produces something more durable: a profession in which the patrol officer and the intelligence analyst are no longer strangers to each other's work. A profession in which the ordinary day—the traffic stop, the neighborhood dispute, the suspicious vehicle—becomes a source of protective intelligence, not just a series of resolved calls. That profession is within reach. The tools are here. The understanding is here. What remains is the decision to teach it.

About the Author

The author spent 27 years in law enforcement in Southern California, starting as a deputy sheriff and retiring as a captain. His breadth of experience, coupled with his higher education, has coalesced into this book. Alongside his law enforcement career, he served 15 years in the military, where intelligence sharing wasn't optional; it was the difference between a mission succeeding and a unit walking into an ambush.

That contrast sharpened during his teaching of in-service officers and criminal justice students. He noticed a concerning gap in training and curriculum. Some are unaware or unsure how their ordinary observations could become part of something larger, something that could stop harm before it happens. That realization became the engine for this book: not just to describe the gap, but to close it where it starts, in the classroom and the training room.

Dr. Nguyen currently teaches at the college level, preparing the next wave of officers and criminal justice professionals. He has seen what works when training is intentional and what fails when it relies on assumptions. This book is his effort to give educators a roadmap—practical, grounded in real agency dynamics, and respectful of civil liberties—for producing officers who don't just react to chaos, but help prevent it. The quiet gap exists. It doesn't have to stay that way.